Needlecraft Kingdom

by Adalee Winter

Copyright © 1975 by Oxmoor House, Inc.
Book Division of the Progressive Farmer Company
P.O. Box 2463, Birmingham, Alabama 35202

Library of Congress Catalog Card Number: 75-32265
ISBN: 0-8487-0413-4

Manufactured in the United States of America

Second Printing 1979

Needlecraft Kingdom

Cover and Interior Photography: Bert O'Neal

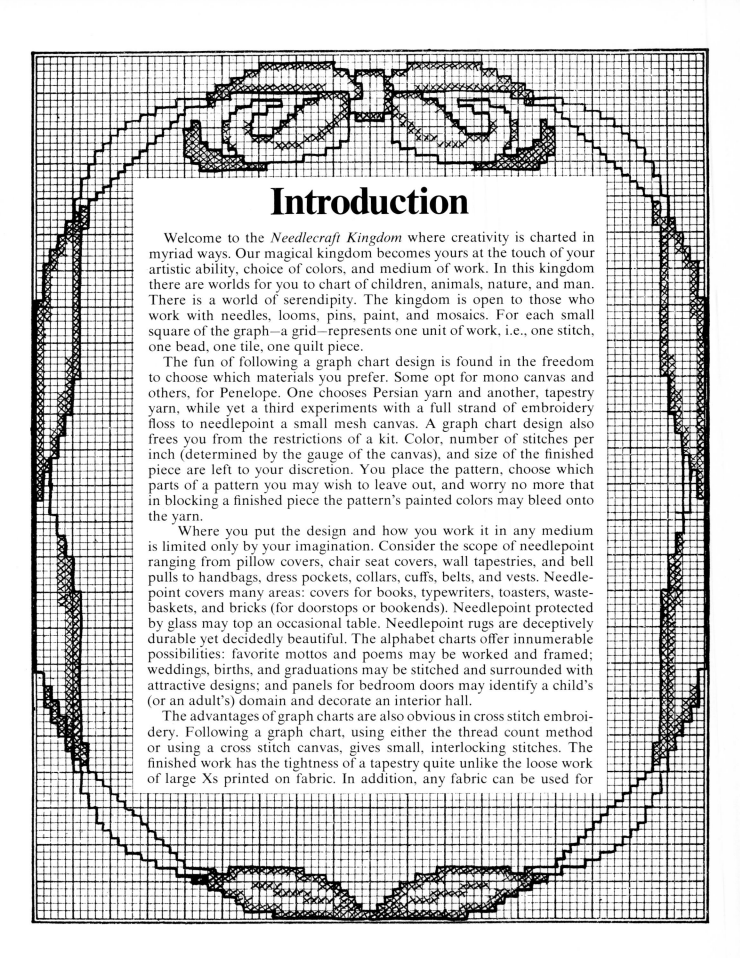

Introduction

Welcome to the *Needlecraft Kingdom* where creativity is charted in myriad ways. Our magical kingdom becomes yours at the touch of your artistic ability, choice of colors, and medium of work. In this kingdom there are worlds for you to chart of children, animals, nature, and man. There is a world of serendipity. The kingdom is open to those who work with needles, looms, pins, paint, and mosaics. For each small square of the graph—a grid—represents one unit of work, i.e., one stitch, one bead, one tile, one quilt piece.

The fun of following a graph chart design is found in the freedom to choose which materials you prefer. Some opt for mono canvas and others, for Penelope. One chooses Persian yarn and another, tapestry yarn, while yet a third experiments with a full strand of embroidery floss to needlepoint a small mesh canvas. A graph chart design also frees you from the restrictions of a kit. Color, number of stitches per inch (determined by the gauge of the canvas), and size of the finished piece are left to your discretion. You place the pattern, choose which parts of a pattern you may wish to leave out, and worry no more that in blocking a finished piece the pattern's painted colors may bleed onto the yarn.

Where you put the design and how you work it in any medium is limited only by your imagination. Consider the scope of needlepoint ranging from pillow covers, chair seat covers, wall tapestries, and bell pulls to handbags, dress pockets, collars, cuffs, belts, and vests. Needlepoint covers many areas: covers for books, typewriters, toasters, wastebaskets, and bricks (for doorstops or bookends). Needlepoint protected by glass may top an occasional table. Needlepoint rugs are deceptively durable yet decidedly beautiful. The alphabet charts offer innumerable possibilities: favorite mottos and poems may be worked and framed; weddings, births, and graduations may be stitched and surrounded with attractive designs; and panels for bedroom doors may identify a child's (or an adult's) domain and decorate an interior hall.

The advantages of graph charts are also obvious in cross stitch embroidery. Following a graph chart, using either the thread count method or using a cross stitch canvas, gives small, interlocking stitches. The finished work has the tightness of a tapestry quite unlike the loose work of large Xs printed on fabric. In addition, any fabric can be used for

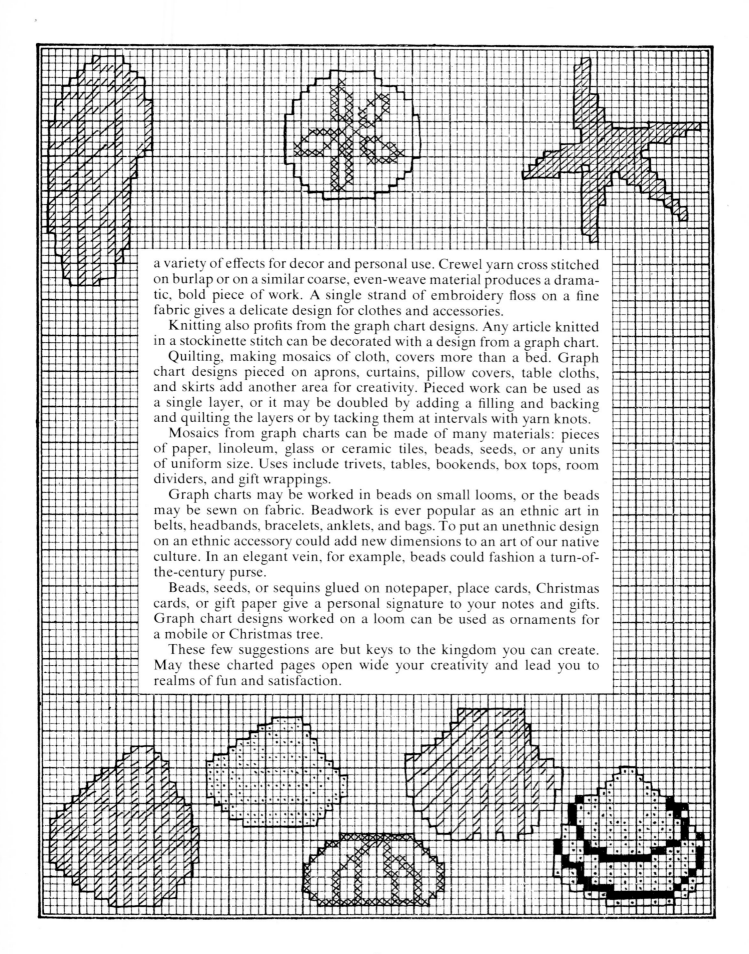

a variety of effects for decor and personal use. Crewel yarn cross stitched on burlap or on a similar coarse, even-weave material produces a dramatic, bold piece of work. A single strand of embroidery floss on a fine fabric gives a delicate design for clothes and accessories.

Knitting also profits from the graph chart designs. Any article knitted in a stockinette stitch can be decorated with a design from a graph chart.

Quilting, making mosaics of cloth, covers more than a bed. Graph chart designs pieced on aprons, curtains, pillow covers, table cloths, and skirts add another area for creativity. Pieced work can be used as a single layer, or it may be doubled by adding a filling and backing and quilting the layers or by tacking them at intervals with yarn knots.

Mosaics from graph charts can be made of many materials: pieces of paper, linoleum, glass or ceramic tiles, beads, seeds, or any units of uniform size. Uses include trivets, tables, bookends, box tops, room dividers, and gift wrappings.

Graph charts may be worked in beads on small looms, or the beads may be sewn on fabric. Beadwork is ever popular as an ethnic art in belts, headbands, bracelets, anklets, and bags. To put an unethnic design on an ethnic accessory could add new dimensions to an art of our native culture. In an elegant vein, for example, beads could fashion a turn-of-the-century purse.

Beads, seeds, or sequins glued on notepaper, place cards, Christmas cards, or gift paper give a personal signature to your notes and gifts. Graph chart designs worked on a loom can be used as ornaments for a mobile or Christmas tree.

These few suggestions are but keys to the kingdom you can create. May these charted pages open wide your creativity and lead you to realms of fun and satisfaction.

The Animal World: rooster pillow in full strand cotton embroidery floss on 12-mesh canvas. *A Child's World:* balloons on child's T-shirt in cross-stitch embroidery; alphabet designs on afghan, crocheted with cross-stitch, and on needlepoint toy block; Tuesday's child design cut into clay tile and glazed. *Four Seasons:* flag in seed beads sewn to Aida cloth. *Geometrics:* piecework pillow.

A Child's World

Legend:

- ■ —brown
- □ —white
- ⊟ —pink
- ⊡ —yellow
- ▨ —deep yellow
- ▨ —yellow green
- ▨ —light green
- ▨ —green
- ▨ —blue green
- ■ —dark blue
- ▨ —blue
- ▨ —light blue

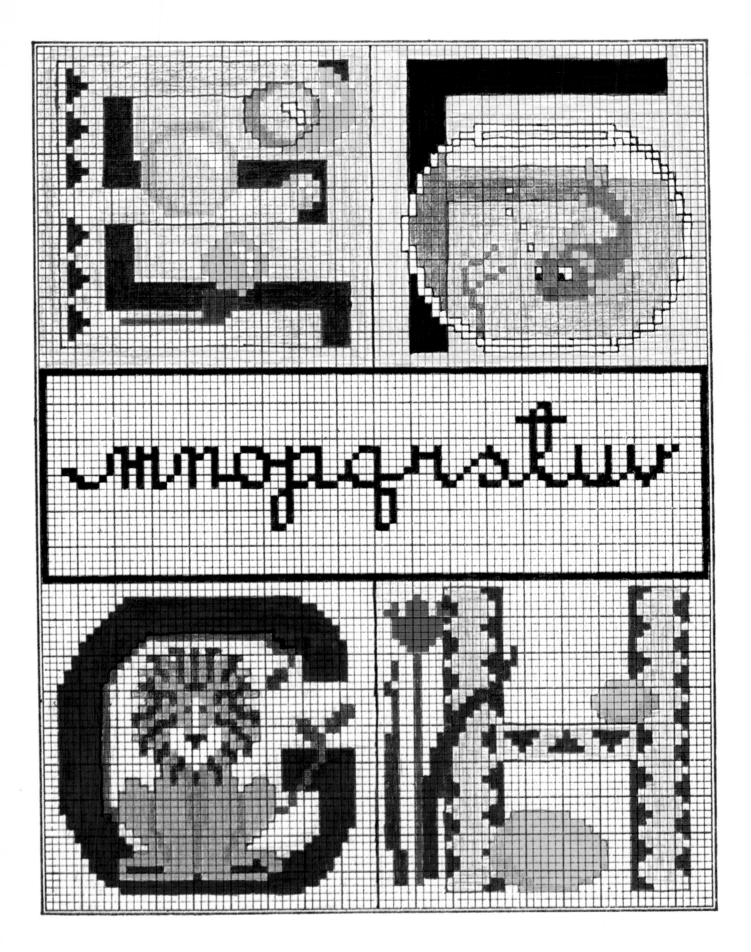

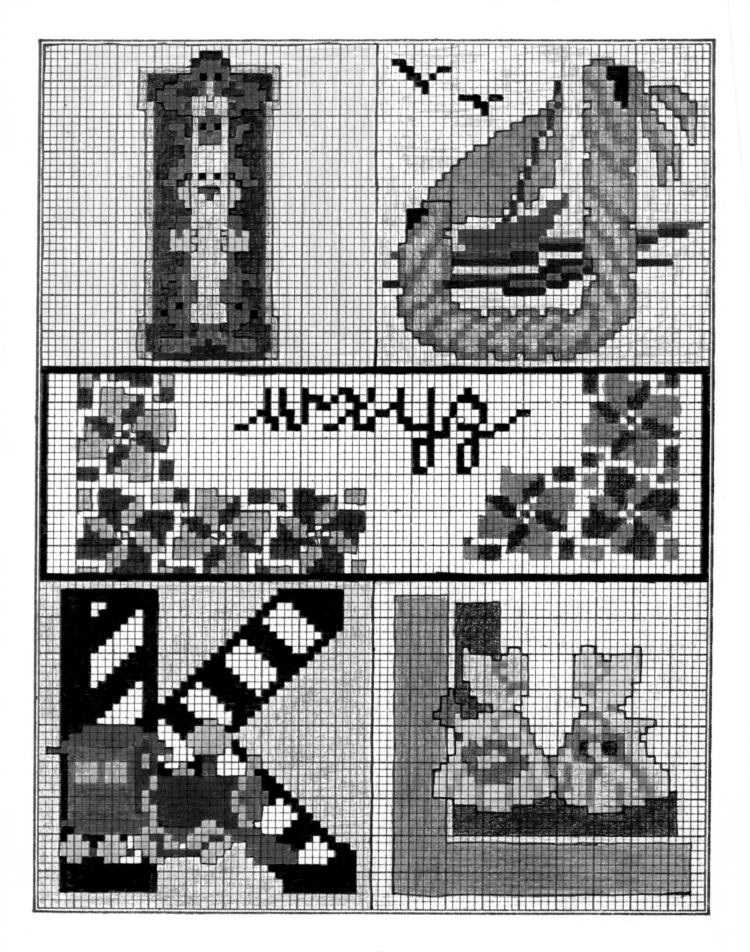

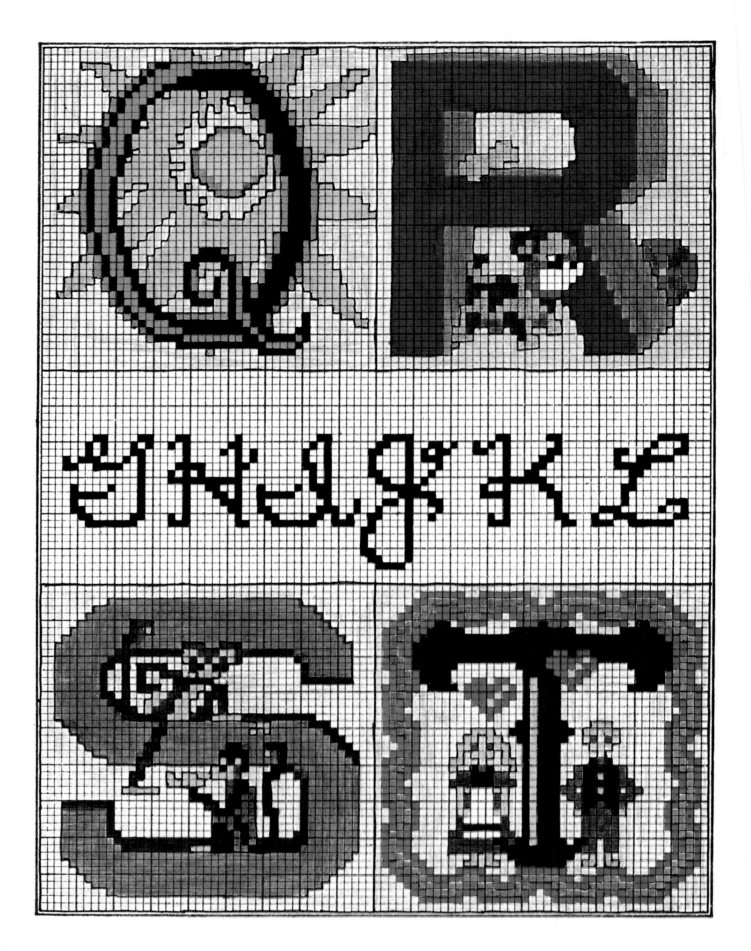

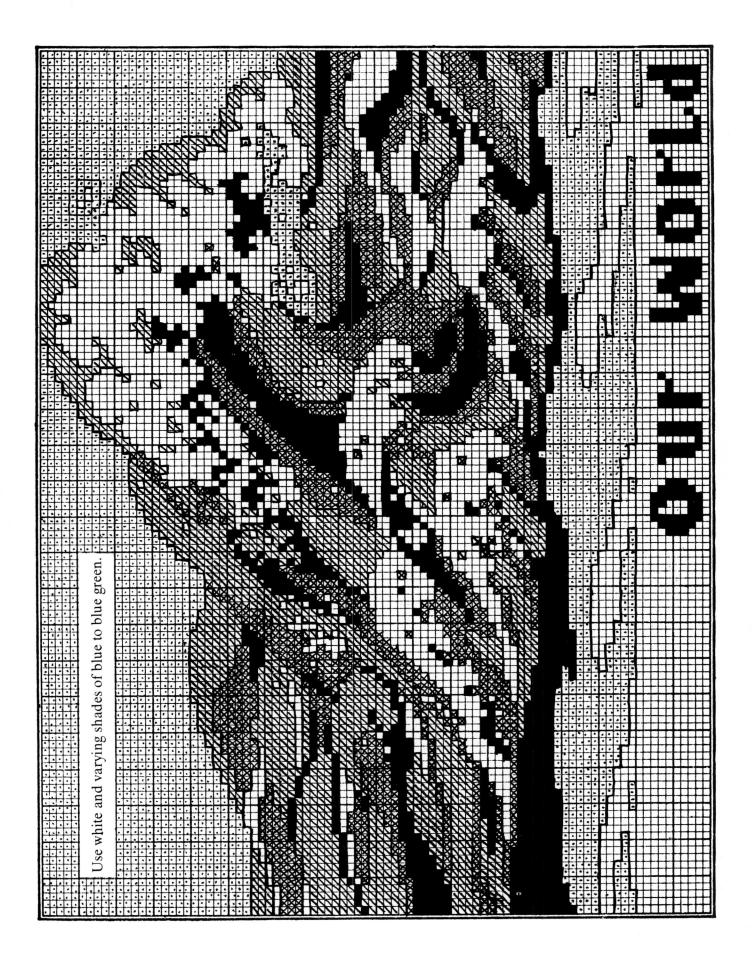

Use white and varying shades of blue to blue green.

Our World

29

31

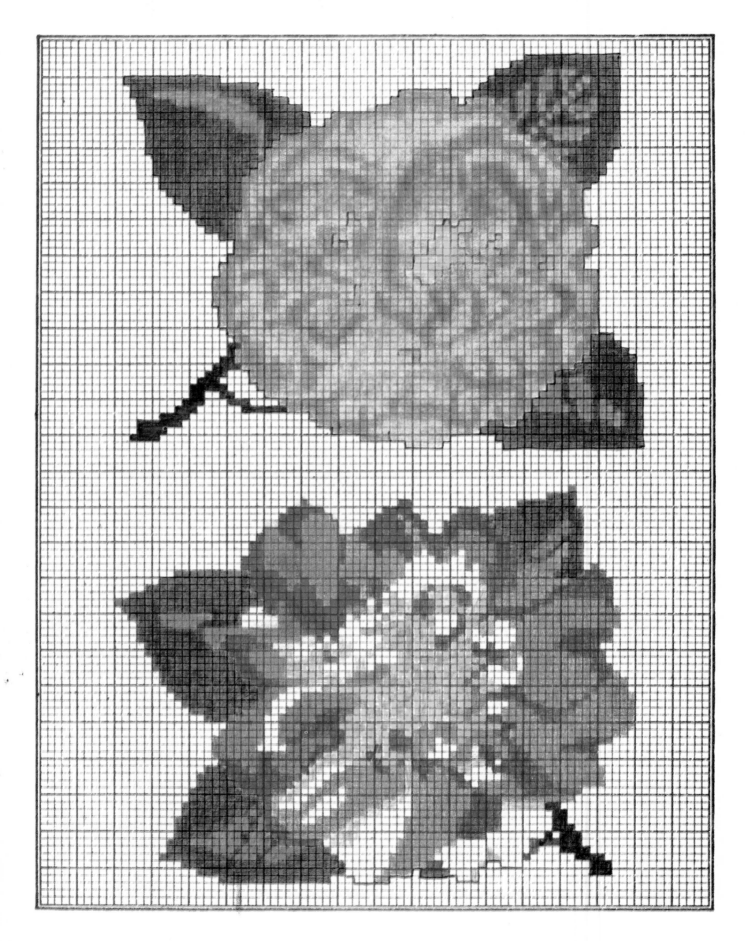

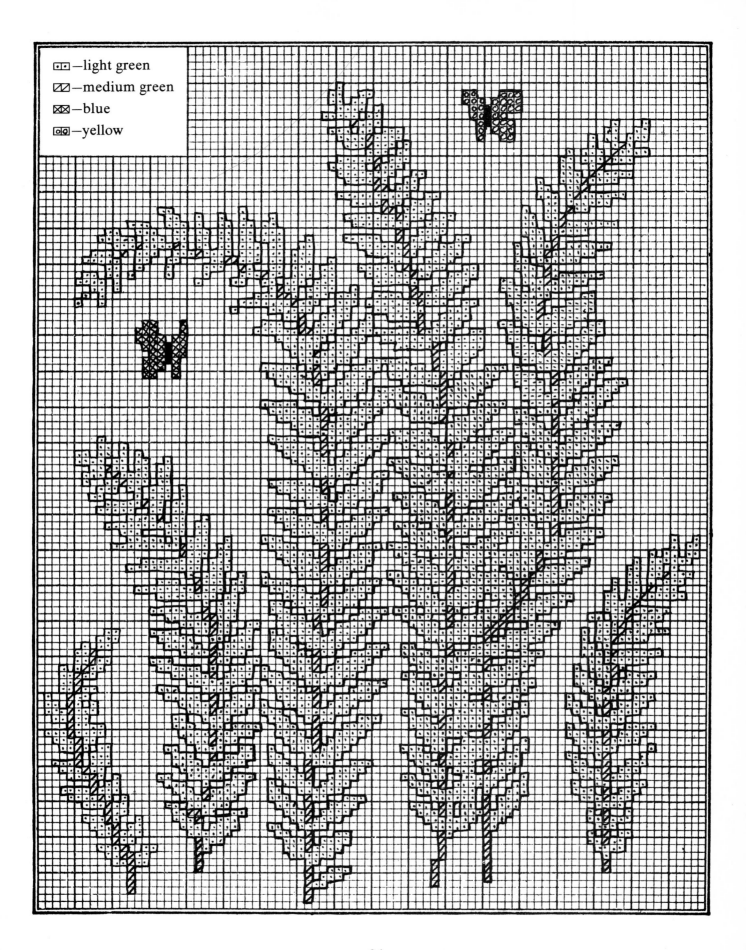

A Child's World: alphabet totem pole design on beadwork pendant necklace. *Four Seasons:* fish tray in glazed mosaics; some designs on Christmas tree skirt. *Geometrics:* sunburst knitted sleeveless pullover; knitted pin cushion. *Serendipity:* Santa tree or package ornament, beads glued to paper; bell tree ornament or lapel pin, beads sewn to Penelope canvas; Christmas tree skirt, cross-stitch embroidery.

36

Use shades of a color such as ⊡ light beige through ⊘ beige, ⊠ light brown and ■ brown; or ⊡ pale gray, ⊘ gray, ⊠ charcoal, and ■ black; or shades of blue or of gold. Shades of two different colors may also be combined in one design.

Around the World

⊏⊐—white

ᴍᴍ—green

⊙⊙—red

The upper right hand corner shows a diagram for working in Bargello. Each stitch covers 4 canvas threads, except where compensating. It will be easier to work with the canvas turned sideways in order that the left side becomes the top and the stitches are worked vertically. Stitches marked —— should be worked in white.

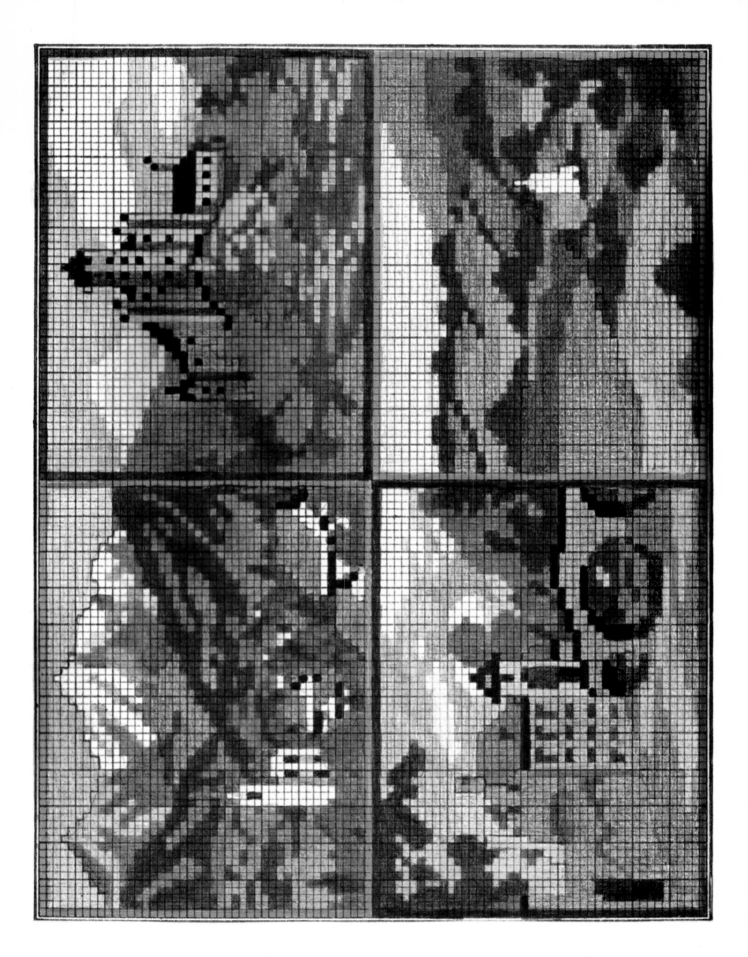

The Animal World: needlepoint flicker pillow. *Around the World:* Oriental tree, glazed mosaic trivet. *A Child's World:* alphabet flowerpot design piecework on seat cover (or wall hanging). *Four Seasons:* snowflake piecework on card table cover. *Our World:* needlepoint fern pillow (or wastebasket cover).

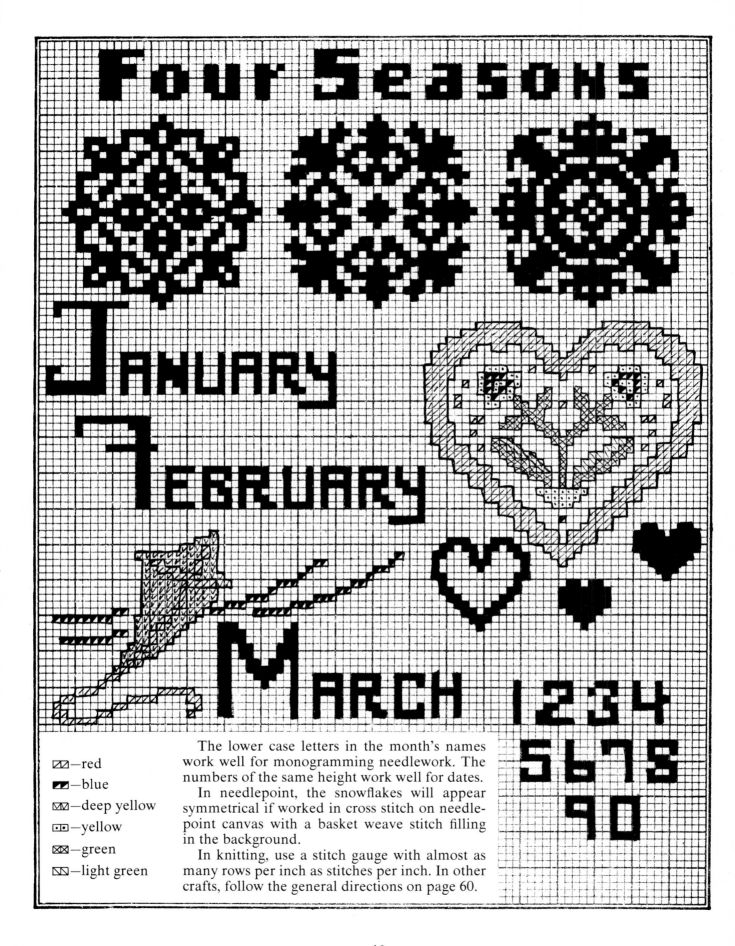

Four Seasons

January

February

March

1234
5678
90

—red
—blue
—deep yellow
—yellow
—green
—light green

The lower case letters in the month's names work well for monogramming needlework. The numbers of the same height work well for dates.

In needlepoint, the snowflakes will appear symmetrical if worked in cross stitch on needlepoint canvas with a basket weave stitch filling in the background.

In knitting, use a stitch gauge with almost as many rows per inch as stitches per inch. In other crafts, follow the general directions on page 60.

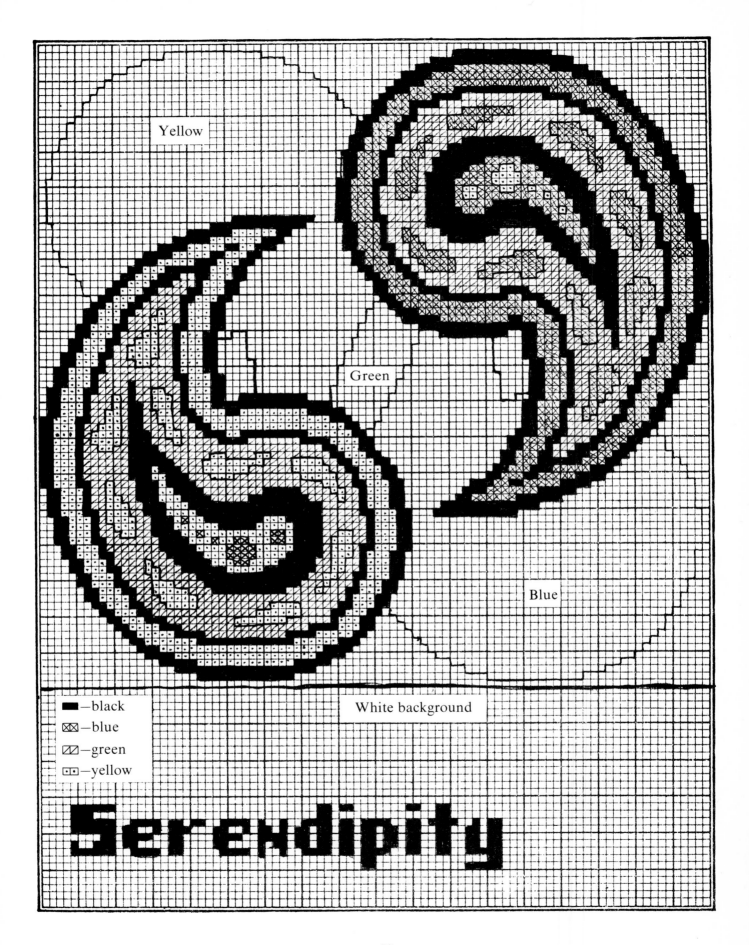

Yellow

Green

Blue

■—black
⊠—blue
▨—green
⊡—yellow

White background

Serendipity

50

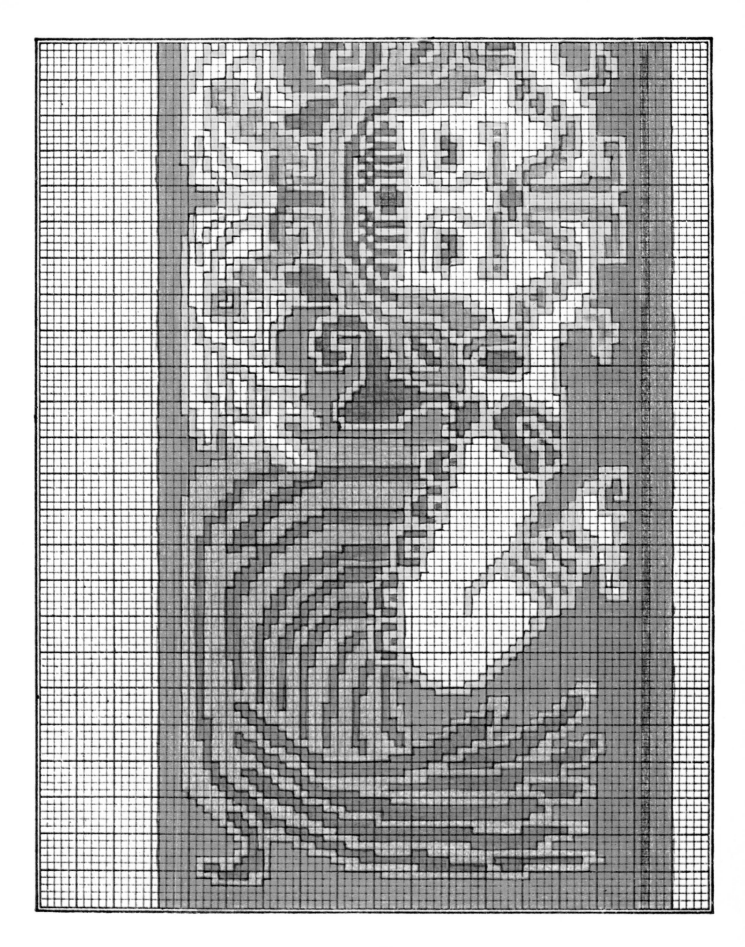

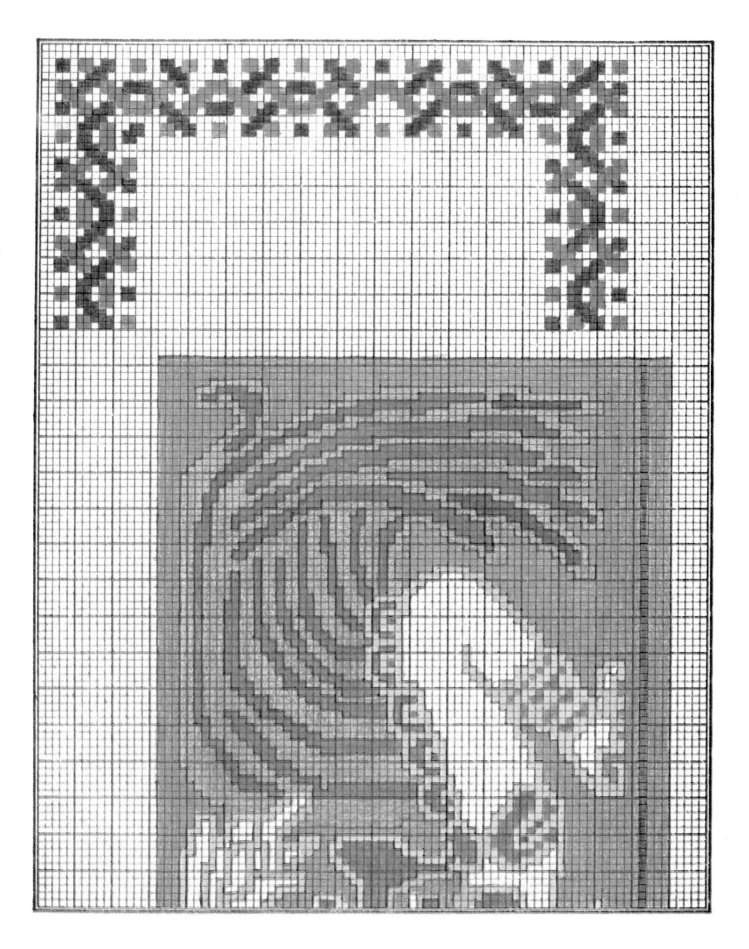

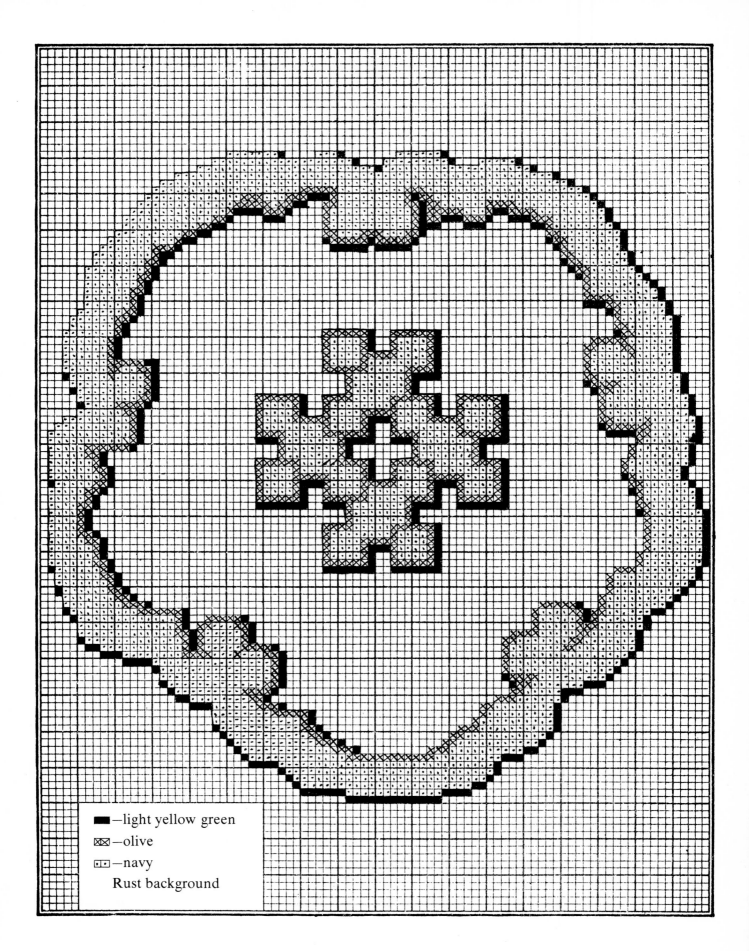

—light yellow green

⊠—olive

⊡—navy

Rust background

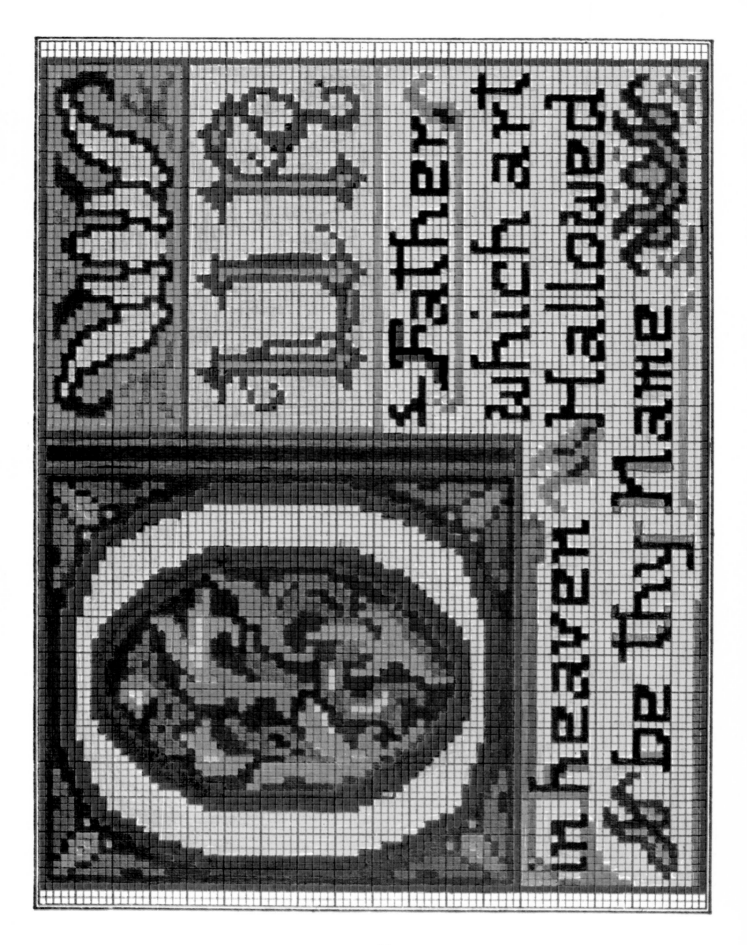

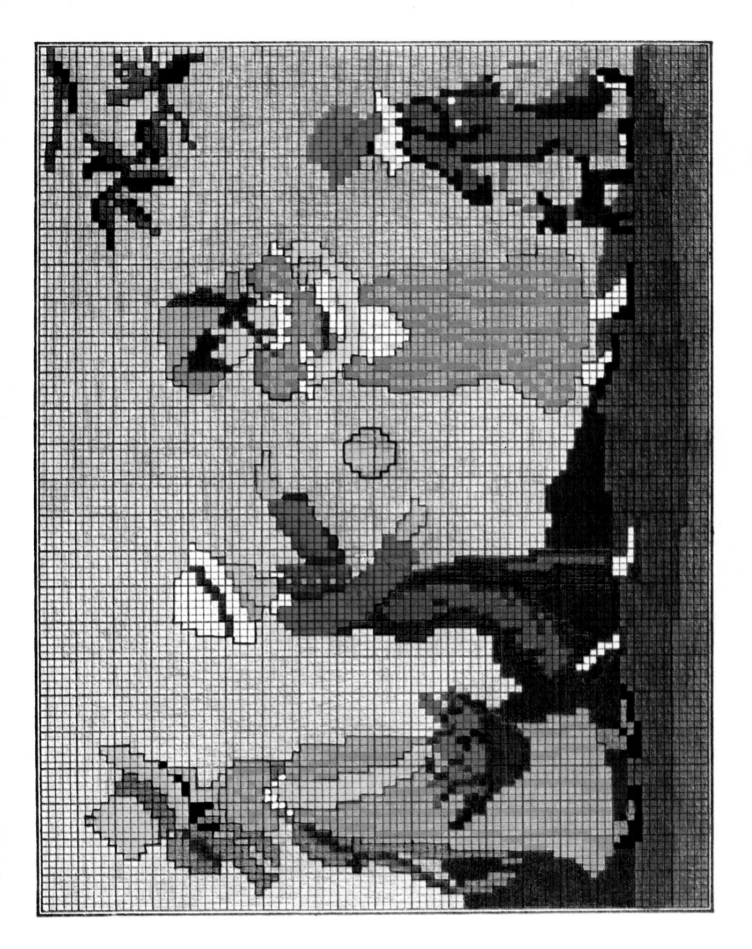

57

motto

Family name

Use colors to correspond to your family's coat of arms.

How To Follow Graph Charts

Each grid or smallest square of the graph represents one unit of work, i.e., one stitch, one bead, one tile.

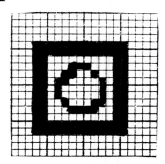

Beadwork: Looms for beadwork are packaged with instructions for following graph charts, or books on beadwork tell how to make a simple loom and follow a graph chart. Also, following a graph chart, you may sew beads onto even-weave cloth or canvas. The seed beads that are used in Indian beadwork are a good size to use on 12- to 14-mesh canvas or fabric. Larger beads may be used for 10-inch gauge canvas or fabric. Since the beads are taller than they are wide, the finished piece will look more narrow than the design on the chart.

Seed beads may be glued with liquid white glue to flat graph paper, using one seed per grid on paper that has 13 grids to the inch. When the glue is dry, cut away the paper around the beads with sharp, curved blade, small scissors. This bead design may then be used as a pin or a pendant; pasted to notepaper, place cards, name tags and such; or used as tree ornaments or in mobiles.

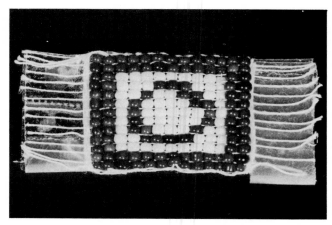

Piecing: All fabric pieces used should be cut square and the same size. Allow at least ¼ inch on each side for seams. Determine the size of the finished work by multiplying the size of one fabric square (minus seam allowances) by the number of grids in a horizontal row and in a vertical row of the design. Piece strips of the fabric squares together to match the horizontal rows of grids of the chart, matching colors and positions. Then sew the strips together so that the seams meet at the corners.

Knitting: Knitted stitches are wider than they are high. Therefore, a design knitted according to a graph chart whose grids are square will look wider and shorter than the design. Choose a size needle and gauge yarn that will give you nearly as many rows per inch as stitches per inch. About every fifth or seventh row, knit a second identical row to be in approximately the same proportion as the design. The design must be worked where there are no increases, decreases, yarn overs, slipped stitches,

or pattern stitches. Knit a gauge swatch to determine what size the knitted design will be. Divide the number of horizontal stitches in an inch into the number of grids in the graph chart design to find how many inches wide the design will be. The number of rows in an inch of the swatch divided into the number of vertical grids in the chart will give the height of the design.

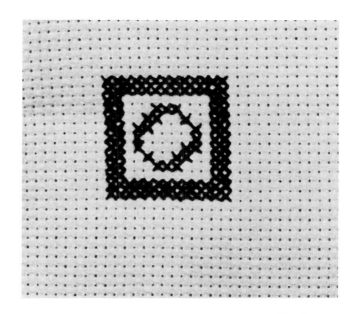

Cross stitch embroidery: Usually only the design part of the graph chart is followed in doing cross stitch embroidery because the fabric is the background. You may work with either an even-weave material or with ravel-out canvas. Divide the number of stitches that will be worked in an inch into the number of grids in the chart to find the number of inches in height and width of the finished embroidery. Find the center grid, or 4 grids, of the chart and the center of the area of the fabric that is to be embroidered. Begin with a center stitch and work out in any direction.

Needlepoint: Determine the size of the canvas needed by dividing the number of vertical threads in an inch of the canvas into the number of vertical grids in the graph chart, (usually 10 or 12 in needlepoint canvas; 5 in rug or quick-point canvas). This will give the number of vertical inches of canvas needed for the design. Divide the same number into the horizontal grids of the chart to determine the width of canvas needed for the design. Allow for background stitches and at least an inch on each side for seam allowance or finishing. Work the design stitches first, using the tent stitch when possible. (The tent stitch is diagrammed and discussed on the following page.) Find the center grid or grids of the graph chart and the center of the canvas. Begin there, counting grids in the chart and stitches on the canvas, working up and matching stitches in color and position to the chart. The background and large areas of the design should be done in the basket weave stitch. Use the half-cross stitch only when necessary to change direction in working the design.

Mosaics: The units used in making a mosaic from a graph chart must be of uniform size and must be able to fit reasonably well into a square. Determine the size of the finished mosaic by multiplying the size of one unit used, such as one tile, by the number of grids in a horizontal row and in a vertical row of the chart. Always work out from the center.

How to Use a Tent Stitch
to Work a Graph Chart Design

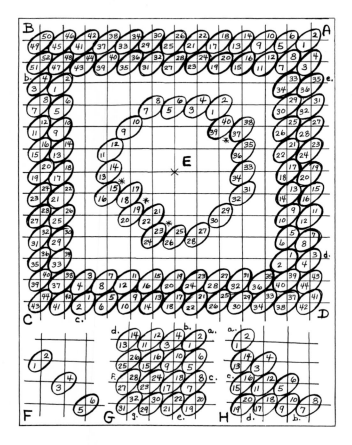

On this page is a diagram for working the tent stitch which is drawn from the small graph chart found on the preceding page. Use this diagram for help in stitching the design only. The background should be done either in the basket weave or a pattern stitch, such as the Scotch diagonal, cashmere, brick, etc.

In needlepoint stitch diagrams, the yarn comes up from underneath the canvas on odd numbers, 1,3,5, etc., and goes down through the canvas to underneath on even numbers, 2,4,6, etc.

The tent stitch may be worked in any direction without turning the canvas. It covers one thread intersection on top of the canvas and two thread intersections underneath. Every needlepoint stitch slants from lower left to upper right and covers one canvas thread intersection on top of the work. Penelope canvas has double threads vertically and horizontally, which are treated as one thread unless the work is petitpoint. The tent stitch requires about 1¼ yards of tapestry yarn for every 100 adjacent stitches. In buying yarn, allow for yarn used for

the beginning and ending of a color and for yarn taken out when errors occur. Avoid using yarn that has been ripped out.

A to B on the diagram shows a double row of tent stitches, working from right to left. Working from top to bottom of the canvas, b. to C shows a double row of tent stitches. Notice that each stitch begins at the end of the same stitch that is nearest the direction in which you are working. In other words, in A-B each stitch begins at the left end of that stitch since you are working toward the left of the canvas. In b.-C each stitch begins at the bottom of the stitch since you are working down the canvas.

From left to right, c.-D is a double row of tent stitches, so each stitch begins at the upper right and goes back to the lower left. A double row of tent stitches going up, d.-e., begins each stitch at the top of that stitch.

The center of the chart, E, should be worked in the tent stitch whenever possible. The stitches marked with an * show that in changing directions of rows of stitches it is sometimes necessary to take 1 half-cross stitch, i.e., a stitch that covers only one thread intersection underneath.

Stitches 7-8, 9-10, 11-12 and stitches 27-28, 29-30, 31-32 show a diagonal row of single stitches running from upper right to lower left and from lower left to upper right. Use this stitch as little as possible.

Running from upper left to lower right, F indicates a single row of diagonal stitches. Spaces will be left between stitches because the slant of the stitch is opposite to the slant of the line of stitches. They will not appear connected as they do on the graph chart or on any needlecraft other than needlepoint. A needlepoint stitch is not square, so it does not meet another stitch at the upper left and lower right. These spaces may be filled in with another stitch in the same color to the right of the first stitch and of each stitch going down, or to the left of the second stitch in the row and of each stitch going down. The charts in this book are drawn so that this problem is avoided as often as is possible.

On the diagram, H shows that the basket weave or diagonal tent stitch may be worked beginning with a row of diagonal stitches, filling in an area to the left of the design, as well as in the traditional basket weave beginning in the upper right corner of the canvas.

The Animal World: count thread embroidery poodle on hardanger cloth with cotton floss. *Serendipity:* needlepoint Quetzelcoatl; needlepoint Peaceable Kingdom; count thread embroidery Victorian children on Aida cloth; needlepoint Christmas stocking.

63

Ways to Use Graph Charts

Coding

Beadwork	B	Mosaics	M
Cross stitch	C	Needlepoint	N
Knitting	K	Piecework	P

Afghan	C, K, P	Name tags	B, C, N
Apron	C, P	Napkins	C
Armband	B, C, K, N	Napkin rings	B, C, K, N
		Notepaper	B, C, M (paper)
Bed cover	C, K, P		
Bell pull	B, C, N	Pendant Necklace	B
Belt	B, C, K, N	Pillow	C, K, N, P
Bench cover	C, P, N	Pillow cases	C
Book cover	C, P, M	Pin Cushion	C, K, N, P
	(paper, decoupaged), N	Place cards	B, C, M
(address, album, baby, Bible, Christmas card		Place mats	C, M (paper,
list, cookbook, photo, scrapbook, telephone,			decoupaged), N
wedding)		Pool bottom	M
Box lid	B, C, M, N		
Brick cover	C, K, N	Quilt	C, K, P
(door stop, bookends)			
		Rug	N
Chair seat	C, P, N	(full or doll house size)	
Checkbook cover	B, C, K, N	Room divider	N
Christmas stocking	C, K, N		
Christmas tree ornament	B, C, K, N	Scarf	C, K
Christmas tree skirt	C, sequins	Small appliance cover	C, N, P
Clutch purse	B, C, K, N	Stuffed toy	C, K, N, P
Coasters	B, C, N		
Curtains	C, P	Tablecloth or cover	C, P
		Tabletop	C or N
Drapery tie backs	C, N	(covered with glass), M	
		Tag	B, C, N
Eyeglass case	B, C, K, N	(decanter, golf bag, key, luggage)	
		Tennis ball pocket	C, N
Footstool	C, N, P	Tennis racquet cover	C, N, P
		Tie (man's)	C, K, N
Game board	C, M, N	Tile floor	M
Garment decoration	C, K, N	Tote bag	C, K, N, P
Gift wrapping paper	M (paper)	Towel	C
Golf club covers	C, N	Trivet	B, C or N
Greeting cards	B, C, M	(covered with glass), M	
	(paper)	Typewriter cover	C, N, P
Handkerchief	C	Vest	C, K, N
Hatband	B, C, K, N		
		Wall	M
Lapel pin	B	Wall hanging, (framed)	C, M, N, P
Legband	B, C, K, N	Wall hanging (unframed)	B, C, M,
Luggage rack straps	C, N		N, P
		Wastebasket cover	C, M (paper),
Mat for framed picture			N, P
or document	B, C, N	Window shade	M, P